J
ALLEN COUNTY PUBLIC LIBRARY
3 1833 04151 1277

FRIENDS OF ACPL

Read-About Geography

MAR 0 1 2002

Africa

By Allan Fowler

Consultant
Nanci R. Vargus, Ed.D.
Primary Multiage Teacher
Decatur Township Scho··· ·· ··dianapolis, Indiana

D1510983

Children's Press®
A Division of Scholastic Inc.
New York   Toronto   London   Auckland   Sydney
Mexico City   New Delhi   Hong Kong
Danbury, Connecticut

Allen County Public Library
900 Webster Street
PO Box 2270
Fort Wayne, IN 46801-2270

Designer: Herman Adler Design
Photo Researcher: Caroline Anderson
The photo on the cover shows two giraffes in Africa's grasslands.

Library of Congress Cataloging-in-Publication Data

Fowler, Allan.
    Africa / by Allan Fowler.
      p. cm. — (Rookie read-about geography)
    Includes index.
    Summary: A simple introduction to the continent of Africa, including
its geographical features.
    ISBN 0-516-22238-4 (lib. bdg.)   0-516-25979-2 (pbk.)
    1. Africa—Juvenile literature. 2. Africa—Geography—Juvenile literature.
[1. Africa.] I. Title. II. Series.
DT3 .F69   2001
960—dc21
                              00-057038

©2001 Children's Press®
A Division of Scholastic Inc.
All rights reserved. Published simultaneously in Canada.
Printed in the United States of America.
1 2 3 4 5 6 7 8 9 10 R 10 09 08 07 06 05 04 03 02 01

The biggest pieces of land on Earth are called continents.

There are seven continents.

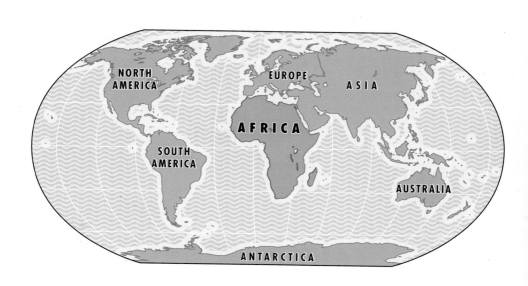

Africa

4

Africa (AF-ri-kuh) is the second largest continent. More than fifty countries make up Africa.

You can find Africa
on a globe.

First, look for the
equator (ee-KWAY-tur).
The equator is the
imaginary line around
the center of the Earth.

equator

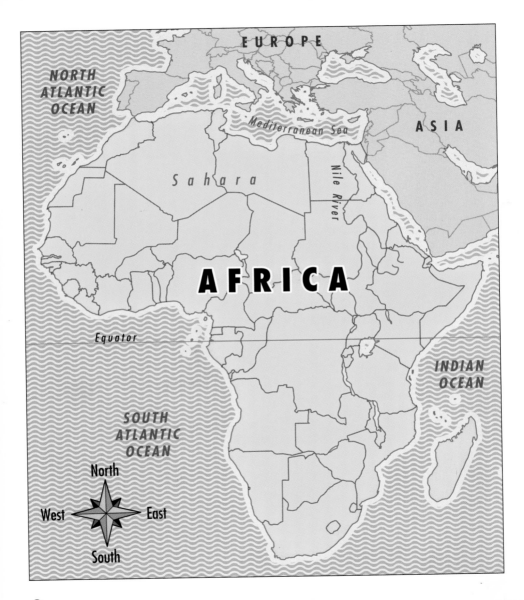

EUROPE

NORTH
ATLANTIC
OCEAN

Mediterranean Sea

ASIA

Sahara

Nile River

AFRICA

Equator

INDIAN
OCEAN

SOUTH
ATLANTIC
OCEAN

North

West   East

South

The equator goes through the middle of Africa. Africa is just below the continent of Europe (YOOR-up).

The Mediterranean (med-i-tuh-RAY-nee-uhn) Sea separates Africa from Europe.

The Sahara Desert takes up most of the top, or north, of Africa. It is the world's biggest desert.

Sand, rocks, and mountains cover the Sahara. Only a few trees and shrubs grow there.

3 1833 04151 1277

Mongooses live in
the Sahara Desert.

Owls live there, too.

The grasslands are below,
or south, of the Sahara.

Zebras and elephants live
in the grasslands.

Birds, such as ostriches (OS-trich-es), also live in the grasslands. Ostriches are too heavy to fly.

Gorillas live in Africa's rain forests. But people have cut down some of these forests.

If we do not protect the gorillas, they may disappear.

The Serengeti (ser-en-GET-ee)
National Park is a safe home
to many African animals.

Giraffe (juh-RAF)

Lions

Some Africans live
in busy cities.

Others live in small villages.

Many people work in offices, stores, or schools.

Office worker

Miner

Some work on farms, in
mines, or on the grasslands
herding cattle.

There are big rivers in Africa. The Nile is the longest river in the world.

If you visit Africa, be sure to stop at Victoria (vik-TOR-ee-uh) Falls.

You can hear the roar of this big waterfall from twenty miles away!

Words You Know

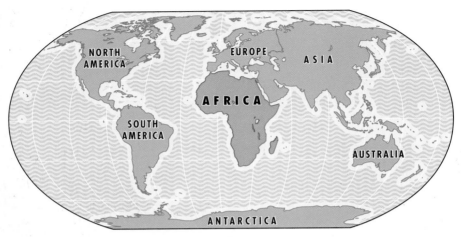

continents

globe

grassland

Nile River

rain forest

Sahara Desert

Serengeti National Park

Victoria Falls

Index

About the Author

Allan Fowler is a freelance writer with a background in advertising.
Born in New York, he now lives in Chicago and enjoys traveling.

Photo Credits

Photographs ©: Corbis-Bettmann: 12 (Sharna Balfour/Gallo Images),
13 (Nigel J. Dennis/Gallo Images), 20, 31 bottom left (Buddy Mays),
24 (Charles O'Rear), 18, 31 top right; Nance S. Trueworthy: 7, 30 bottom
left; Photo Researchers, NY: 17 (Tim Davis), 11, 31 center left (Englebert),
23 (Georg Gerster), 14 (Stephen J. Krasemann), 4 (Tom Van Sant/Geosphere
Project, Santa Monica/SPL), 15, 30 bottom right (Art Wolfe); Stone: cover
(Daryl Balfour), 22 (John Chard), 21 (Johnny Johnson), 25, 29, 31 bottom right
(Ian Murphy), 26, 31 top left (Hugh Sitton).

Maps by Bob Italiano.